CW00497103

On the Accuracy of Nielsen Homescan Data

Economic Research Service (ERS), United States
Department of Agriculture (USDA), Liran Einav

The BiblioGov Project is an effort to expand awareness of the public documents and records of the U.S. Government via print publications. In broadening the public understanding of government and its work, an enlightened democracy can grow and prosper. Ranging from historic Congressional Bills to the most recent Budget of the United States Government, the BiblioGov Project spans a wealth of government information. These works are now made available through an environmentally friendly, print-on-demand basis, using only what is necessary to meet the required demands of an interested public. We invite you to learn of the records of the U.S. Government, heightening the knowledge and debate that can lead from such publications.

Included are the following Collections:

Budget of The United States Government
Presidential Documents
United States Code
Education Reports from ERIC
GAO Reports
History of Bills
House Rules and Manual
Public and Private Laws

Code of Federal Regulations
Congressional Documents
Economic Indicators
Federal Register
Government Manuals
House Journal
Privacy act Issuances
Statutes at Large

United States
Department
of Agriculture

Economic
Research
Service

Economic
Research
Report
Number 69

December 2008

On the Accuracy of Nielsen Homescan Data

Liran Einav
Ephraim Leibtag
Aviv Nevo

Photo credit: Shutterstock

United States
Department
of Agriculture

Economic
Research Report
Number 69

December 2008

A Report from the Economic Research Service

www.ers.usda.gov

On the Accuracy of Nielsen Homescan Data

Liran Einav

Ephraim Leibtag

Aviv Nevo

Abstract

Researchers use Nielsen Homescan data, which provide detailed food-purchase information from a panel of U.S. households, to address a variety of important research topics.
However, some question the credibility of the data since the data are self-recorded
and the recording process is time-consuming. Matching purchase records from 2004
Homescan data with data obtained from a large grocery retailer, it is evident that quantities purchased are reported more accurately in Homescan than are prices. Many of the
price differences may be driven by the way Nielsen imputes prices: when available,
Nielsen uses store-level prices instead of the actual price paid by the household. There
are also differences by houshold type in the tendency to make mistakes that are correlated with demographic variables. However, the fraction of variance explained by the
documented recording errors is in line with other research data sets for which cross-vali-
dation studies have been conducted.

Keywords: Nielsen, Homescan, scanner data, validation study

Acknowledgments

The authors would like to thank Andrea Pozzi and Chris Taylor for their research assis-
tance and Oral Capps, Andrea Carlson, Helen Jensen, and Jessica Todd for their helpful
reviewer comments. This research was funded by a cooperative agreement between the
ERS and Northwestern University.

About the Authors

Liran Einav is an associate professor of economics at Stanford University, Ephraim
Leibtag is an economist with ERS, and Aviv Nevo is a professor of economics at
Northwestern University. Einav and Nevo are affiliated with the National Bureau of
Economic Research (NBER), Cambridge, MA.

Contents

Recommended citation format for this publication:

Einav, Liran, Ephraim Leibtag, and Aviv Nevo. *On the Accuracy of Nielsen Homescan Data.* ERR-69, U.S. Dept. of Agriculture, Econ. Res. Serv. December 2008.

Summary

Researchers use Nielsen Homescan data, which provide detailed food-purchase information from a panel of U.S. households, to study the dynamics of retail food markets.

What Is the Issue?

Some questions have been raised regarding the credibility of the Nielsen Homescan data because the data are self-recorded and the recording process is time-consuming. Given the time commitment, households who agree to participate in the sample might not be representative of the U.S. population as a whole, and those who agree to participate may not record their purchases accurately.

What Did the Study Find?

The analysis conducted in this report suggests that the Homescan data contain recording errors in several dimensions, but that the overall accuracy of self-reported data by Homescan panelists seems to be in line with other commonly used (government-collected) economic data sets.

For approximately 20 percent of food-shopping trips recorded in the Nielsen Homescan data, there was no corresponding transaction in the retailer's data, suggesting that either the store or date information was recorded with error. Using the retailer's loyalty card information, the study finds some shopping trips that did not match up with Nielsen Homescan data, implying that households did not record all of their trips in their Homescan records.

For the trips that did match up, roughly 20 percent of the items purchased were not recorded. For those items that were recorded, quantity was reported fairly accurately: 94 percent of the quantity information matched in the two data sets. The match for prices was lower: in almost half of the cases, the two data sets did not agree. However, much of this difference can be attributed to transactions that involved promotional or other temporary sale prices in either the Nielsen Homescan data or the retailer's data.

Nielsen's practice of using store-level data as an estimate of what households actually paid poses a challenge when those stores have multiple possible prices in a given time period due to loyalty card or other shopper-specific price promotions. Indeed, for prices that involve no promotion or temporary price reduction, there are recording errors in only about 17 percent of the cases. Therefore, much of the overall price difference is likely caused by the way Nielsen imputes prices and not by recording errors by the panelists. Mismatched prices would most likely be less of a problem for stores that only have one price per product in a given week, so that the results highlight the importance of store pricing practices in food price analysis.

The study also compares the recording errors to errors in other commonly used economic data sets, and finds that errors in Homescan are of the same order of magnitude, for example, as reporting errors in earnings and employment-status data.

How Was the Study Conducted?

Homescan records contain all products purchased by a household on a particular day in a particular store, as they were scanned by the consumer. The study compared these records to data obtained from a single retailer. The retailer's data contain the products purchased in each of the transactions at the same store and day reported by the household, as recorded by the cashier. Using data from trips made during 2004, the records from both data sets were matched. The matched transactions were compared and contrasted, and differences in various dimensions were recorded. In order to study the impact the recording errors might make in an applied study, the price paid was regressed on household characteristics in both data sets to see if the results differ.

Introduction

Nielsen Homescan data provide rich information about household purchasing patterns that allows researchers to study questions that cannot be addressed using other forms of data. For example, Homescan data cover purchases at retailers such as Wal-Mart and Whole Foods that traditionally do not cooperate with scanner data collection companies. In addition, due to their national coverage, Homescan data provide wide variation in household location and demographics, in contrast to other retail research panels, in which most households are from a small number of markets with relatively limited variation in demographics.

However, questions have been raised about the credibility of the Homescan data since the data are self-recorded and the recording process is time-consuming. One concern is potential sample selection. Given the time commitment, the households who agree to participate in the sample might not be representative of the population of interest. A second concern is that the households who agree to participate in the sample might record their purchases incorrectly.

In this study, we used a unique data set from a single retailer to examine the second concern. We constructed a data set to allow the matching of records from the Nielsen Homescan data with detailed transaction-level data from the retailer. Thus, we were able to observe the same transaction twice—as it was recorded by the retailer, just before the items left the store, and as it was recorded by the Homescan panelist, just after the items reached the house. By comparing the two data sources, we are able to identify three types of potential inaccuracies in the Homescan data:

- if the household did not report a trip to the retailer or misrecorded the trip information (store and date)

- within a trip, if the household did not record, or misrecorded, the product (universal product code, or UPC) information

- for a given product, document misreporting of the price, quantity, and deal information.

This study has multiple purposes. First, we documented the accuracy of Homescan data, by describing the magnitude of mistakes for each of the aforementioned potential recording errors. Second, we investigated whether and how errors are correlated with household or trip characteristics, which would be suggestive of which type of analysis would be more sensitive to such errors, and how. For example, we ask whether a correlation between a price "paid" and demographics could be driven by systematic measurement errors. Third, we plan to use the results of this analysis to suggest adjustments to the use of the data that would make analysis less prone to recording errors[2].

Before looking at the data in more detail, it is important to clarify terminology. First, the retailer's data are treated as the "truth," allowing any differences between the data sets to be attributed to "errors" or "mistakes." Of course, to the extent that there are recording errors in the retailer's data, these words should be interpreted accordingly. We discuss this further in the

[1]See Aguiar and Hurst (2007), Broda and Weinstein (2007), and Hausman and Leibtag (2007) for academic research that relied heavily on Nielsen Homescan data

[2]More generally, the study offers an opportunity to cross validate self-reported data. This has been done for other data sets. Bound et al. (2001) surveyed similar work on validation studies, primarily in the context of the PSID (Panel Study of Income Dynamics).

context of the results. The second terminology issue relates to what is meant by "errors" or "misrecording" in the Homescan data. This issue could be driven by various mechanisms: recording errors by the Homescan panelists themselves, misunderstanding of instructions or errors that are generated due to the way Nielsen puts together its data. This latter case seems most important for the price variable, but overall, the use of "errors," "mistakes," or "misrecording" means any of the possible mechanisms.

Data Sources

Homescan

The Nielsen Homescan data consist of a panel of households who record their grocery purchases. The purchases can come from a wide variety of store types, including traditional food stores, supercenters and warehouse clubs, and online merchants. Interested consumers who are 18 or older register online to participate (at http://www.homescan.com) and are asked to supply demographic information. Based on this information, Nielsen contacts a subset of the registered consumers to become panel members. They are not paid in currency for participating in the program, but every week a panel member who scans at least one purchase receives a set amount of points. The points can be redeemed for merchandise. Panelists can earn additional points for answering surveys and by participating in sweepstakes that are open only to panel members.

The data used was for trips made during 2004. The original data consisted of two panels. Members of the larger set of households, the "61K panel," recorded all UPC-coded food purchases. A subset of these households, the "15K panel," also recorded non-UPC coded products including fresh food purchases and other random weight items, such as fruit and vegetables). In what follows the focus is on the larger panel.

Each participating household was provided with a scanner. As part of setting up the scanner, the households recorded the stores they usually visit. For each shopping trip, the panelist recorded the date and the store, ideally from one of the previously programmed outlets. They then scanned the barcodes of the products they purchased, and entered the quantity of each item, whether the item was purchased at the regular or promotional ("deal") price, and the coupon amount (if used) associated with this purchase.

Nielsen then matches the barcode, or UPC, with detailed product characteristics. The recording of price will turn out to be particularly important for this study. If the household purchased products at a store covered in the Nielsen store-level data ("ScanTrack")—and we think (but could not verify) that all stores operated by the retailer who provided us with the data are covered in the store-level data—Nielsen did not require the household to enter the price paid for each item, in an effort to make the scanning process less time-consuming for the household. Instead, Nielsen imputes the price from the store-level data. To construct this price, we understand that Nielsen uses the average weekly price paid at the store for the corresponding item (UPC). If the same item could be transacted at different prices within the same store during the same week, this imputation process can introduce errors into the price data. A common reason for such price variation across transactions (of the same item within a store-week) is loyalty-card discounts that are only applied to the subset of consumers who use cards. Unless all consumers always use the card, the imputed price is unlikely to be the exact price paid by the consumer. This imputation leads to frequent, sometimes large, price reporting errors.[3,4]

[3]Coupon use itself does not cause this problem. If the consumer purchased the product using a coupon, this value is reported in Homescan and can be subtracted from the reported price to get the actual consumer cost.

[4]For stores that are not covered by the store-level data, Nielsen asks households to report the price paid and checks the prices entered by consumers by comparing them to a range of prices observed elsewhere for the same or similar item. (We think those stores are not in our sample.) If a price is considered out of range, the median regional price is used instead. As an additional validity check, Nielsen also manually reviews transactions with high quantities and households who are at the top of the expenditure distribution in each category.

Retailer's data

The second data set comes from a large national grocery chain, hereafter referred to as the retailer. This retailer records all the transactions in all its stores. For each transaction, the data record the exact time of the transaction, the cashier number, and the loyalty card number, if one was used. The data also list the UPCs purchased, the quantity purchased of each product, the price paid, and information regarding discounts (loyalty card discounts, coupons, etc.). The retailer also links loyalty cards that belong to members of the same household, primarily by matching the street addresses and telephone numbers individuals use when applying for a loyalty card. The retailer then assigns each household a unique identification number. Clearly, this definition of a household is more prone to errors compared to Homescan's definition, in which a household is simply associated with the house at which the scanner resides.

Data Construction

The main challenge in constructing the data was to match transactions and households, as recorded by Homescan, with corresponding transactions and loyalty card numbers, as recorded by the retailer. We matched records between the two data sets in two steps. We first obtained complete transaction level data from the retailer for stores and dates when a household in the Homescan data recorded a visit to the retailer store, and we developed a simple algorithm to match between the purchases recorded in the Homescan data and one of the many transactions recorded in the retailer's data (on that day at that store). We then asked the retailer for the full set of transactions recorded by the holders of the loyalty cards associated with these matched transactions. Figure 1 provides a schematic chart that sketches the key steps in the data construction process. Below we describe this process in more detail. Some readers may find it useful to skip these nitty-gritty details, and go directly to the end of the section, where we summarize the final data set we ended up using.

First Step

For the first step, the objective was to maximize the number of matched transactions given size limitations. These size limitations arise because, without additional information, we needed to have a complete transaction record from a particular store on a particular date for each potential matched transaction. The size of the data file containing this information was about three megabytes, and due to constraints imposed by the retailer, we had to limit this step to roughly 1,500 store-day transaction-level records.

Figure 1
Stages in the data construction process

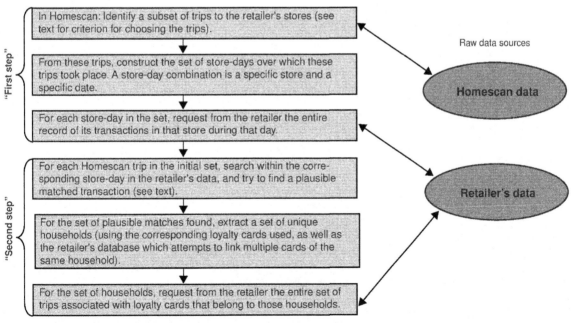

Source: Authors' calculations using Homescan and retailer data.

We therefore proceeded as follows. First, we restricted the data set to two metropolitan areas in which the retailer has high market share. This resulted in a total of 265 different retailer stores (147 in one area, and 118 in the other). The focus on two areas helped in obtaining more data, given the way the retailer organizes its data. Using areas with high market share of the retailer was also useful, as it could raise the probability that a single store-day record would help to match more than a single shopping trip. This would happen if two households in the Homescan panel visited the same store on the same day, which is more likely when the market share of the retailer is high. Since we identify the store by its ZIP code, we also restricted attention to retailer stores that are the only retailer stores in the same ZIP code. This eliminated 76 stores (29 percent), and left a total of 189 stores (101 in one area, 88 in the other).

We then searched the Homescan data for shopping trips at these stores, with the additional conditions that: (1) the trip includes purchase of at least five distinct UPCs (to make a match easier); (2) the trip occurred after February 15, 2004 (to guarantee that the retailer, who deletes transaction-level data older than 2 years, still had these data); and (3) the household shopped at the retailer's stores more than 20 percent and less than 80 percent of its trips, according to Homescan. These trips were made by 342 distinct households in the Homescan data. For 240 of those households, a single trip was randomly selected for each of them. For the remaining 102 households, which included households with at least 10, and not more than 20, reported trips in Homescan data, we selected all their trips. We then requested from the retailer the full transaction records for the store-days that matched those 1,779 trips. Since 74 of these trips were to the same store on the same date, we expected to get 1,705 store-day transaction-level records.

We eventually got 1,603 of those 1,705 requested store-days[5] (1,247 in the first area, 356 in the other). They accounted for 4,080,770 shopping trips and included 122 distinct stores (74 in the first area, and 48 in the other). The 1,603 store-days are associated with 1,675 trips from the sample of 1,779 shopping trips described above. However, as already mentioned, since the retailer enjoys high market share in both areas, it is not surprising that the 1,603 store-day transaction-level data records we obtained are associated with additional 904 trips in Homescan. Given the way we constructed the sample, however, many of these additional trips include a small number of items, or households that rarely shop at the retailer's stores.

Second Step

After obtaining the data from the first step, we developed a simple algorithm to find likely matches between transactions in the Homescan data with transactions in the retailer's data. These likely matches were only used to speed up the data construction process. The data were analyzed later using a more systematic matching procedure. The algorithm used the first five UPCs in the Homescan trip, and declared a match if at least three of these five were found in a given trip in the retailer's data. This algorithm was used with the data we obtained in the first step and found 1,372 likely matches that, according to the Homescan data, were associated with 293 distinct households. Of these

[5]The 102 store-days we did not get were missing at random, due to computer-related technical reasons at the retailer's end.

households, 166 were associated with more than one likely match, and 105 with four or more.

We then asked the retailer to use the loyalty card used in these 1,372 shopping trips and to provide us with all the transactions available for the households associated with these cards (in the retailer's data during the year 2004). Only two of the requested trips were not associated with loyalty cards. For the rest, we obtained all the transactions associated with the same loyalty card and additional transactions that were associated with loyalty cards used by the same household, as classified by the retailer. Since associating multiple cards with the same household did not necessarily match perfectly, the analysis used both the card level and the household level.

In this step, we obtained a total of 40,036 shopping trips from the retailer. These 40,036 trips were associated with 384 distinct stores (139 in the first area, 109 in the second, and 136 in other areas), with 682 distinct loyalty cards (472 in the first area, 203 in the second, and 7 in other areas), and with 529 distinct households, according to the retailer's definition (380 in the first area, 140 in the other).[6] Finally, the 40,036 trips were associated with 34,316 unique store-date-loyalty card combinations, 33,744 unique store-data-household combinations (using the retailer's definition of a household), and 27,746 unique store-date-household combinations, using the Homescan definition. Of these trips, 3,884 (9.7 percent) occurred in a store-day already appearing in the data we obtained earlier, and therefore were one of the 4,080,770 trips obtained in the first step. The 3,884 trips were associated with 3,514 unique store-date-loyalty card combinations, 3,477 unique store-date-household combinations, using the retailer definition, and 2,838 unique store-date-household combinations, using the Homescan definition. The algorithm used to request these data was geared to find likely matches, and therefore may have also found wrong matches. This is one reason that the number of households we intended to match (291, the original 293 minus two that had no associated loyalty cards) was less than the number of households associated with these trips. A second reason may be multiple cards used by the same household that are not linked to each other by the retailer.

Summary

To summarize, we have two different data sets from the retailer. The first data set included full transaction records of 1,603 distinct store-days. In these data, transactions were not associated with a loyalty card. The second data set included 40,036 transactions, which were associated with particular loyalty cards and households. 3,884 of these transactions overlap and appear in both data sets. The first data set was designed to match multiple transactions of 102 households in the Homescan data, and isolated transactions of other households. The second data set was designed to match all transactions of a few hundred households.

[6]Most households and card holders shopped in more than a single store. We associated a household or a card holder with the main store where either shopped. Card holders could be in other areas and appeared in the data only if they were associated with households that are in one of the two areas we focused on.

Record-Matching Strategy

Having obtained the retailer's data, we now describe our strategy for matching records from Homescan with the data obtained from the retailer. Earlier we mentioned a "quick and dirty" matching algorithm we used for the data construction. This was only used to speed up the data requesting process from the retailer, and we do not use its results further. In this section we describe a more systematic matching strategy. It is used for the rest of the study.

We start by analyzing possible matches in the data obtained in the first step. Recall that a Homescan record contains all products purchased by the household on a particular day in a particular store. The retailer's data contain the products purchased in each of the (more than 2,500 on average) shopping trips at the same store and day reported by the household. The goal was to match the Homescan trip to exactly one of the trips in the retailer's data, or to determine that none of the trips in the retailer's data was a good match (which would be indicative of the household not recording the trip in Homescan or possibly recording the trip but misrecording the date or the store).

Since this procedure relies on the coding of the items (UPCs), there was a concern that certain items, especially non-packaged items, might have had different codes at the retailer's stores and at Homescan. An additional concern was that the data used in this report only included the food items scanned by the household, while the store data included nonfood items purchased as well. To deal with these concerns, we generated the universe of UPCs used by Homescan panelists in our entire data and, separately, the universe of UPCs that were used by the retailer in our entire data. We then restricted attention to only the intersection of these two lists of UPCs by eliminating from the analysis all data related to UPCs not in the intersection. In other words, in the analysis below, if a certain UPC in, say, the retailer's data could not be matched to the Homescan data; it is not because it could not have been matched: there is at least one Homescan household who transacted and recorded the same UPC. We should also note that this step also makes the distinction between the "61K panel" households in Homescan and the "15K panel" households mentioned above unimportant. With negligible exceptions, all UPCs that the 15K-panel households were required to scan are non-packaged items, for which the retailer uses a different coding, and were therefore unmatchable.

After reducing the data set as described above, we continue as follows. For each shopping trip in the Homescan data, for which we have the retailer's data for that store and that day, and for each potential trip from the retailer's data, in the same date and store, we count the number of distinct UPCs that overlap. For each of these Homescan trips we keep the two trips (in the retailer's data) with the largest number of UPC overlaps, and define ratios between the UPC overlap in each trip and the number of distinct UPCs in the Homescan trip. The first, r_1, was the ratio of the number of overlapping UPCs in the retailer trip with the highest overlap to the total number of distinct UPCs reported in the Homescan trip. The higher this ratio, the higher the fraction of products matched, and the more likely that this trip was a correct match. The second ratio, r_2, was similar, but was computed for the retailer trip with the second-highest overlap. By construction, r_2 will be less or equal to r1. A higher r_2 makes it more likely that the second trip was also a reasonable match. Since, in reality, there was, at most, a single trip that should be matched, this statistic tries to guard against a false positive. Confidence in the match between the Homescan record and the first trip increased the higher r_1 and the lower r_2 were. In practice it turns out that false positives resulting from this algorithm did not seem to be a concern once the trip included a large number of distinct UPCs.

Using these two statistics, r_1 and r_2, and the number of products purchased during a trip (according to Homescan), each trip in the Homescan data was separated into one of three categories: reliable matches, matches that with high probability did not have a match, and uncertain matches (i.e., we cannot classify these trips into either of the other groups with a reasonable level of certainty). The first group of transactions was used to study the quality of the price and quantity data. The second group was used to document unrecorded trips or errors in recording trip information. We applied different criteria to define the three groups and to verify that all the findings were robust to reasonable modifications of these criteria.[7]

Matching records with the trips reported in the second step was a different problem. Here we were not supplied with a list of all trips recorded in the retailer's data for the day and store. Instead, we are given a single trip that the retailer believed represented the household's purchases on that day. Thus, the matching problem here was not which trip (out of many) matches the Homescan trip, but rather whether a given trip was a good match or not. We do this by computing the ratio r_1, which was, as before, the number of distinct UPCs that overlap divided by the number of items in the Homescan data. Using the statistic r_1 and the total number of distinct items purchased, we classified the Homescan trips into three categories, as was done with the first step data. In principle, in this step the thresholds for r_1 used to classify the trips could have been different than the thresholds used in the first step. It turns out, however, that the vast majority of r_1's that were computed were either close to one or close to zero, making the choice of a threshold irrelevant. As an additional guard against false positives, we also report some of the results when eliminating from the data certain households that seem to be inconsistent in the way they use their loyalty cards.

Results

We used the matched data to quantify the importance of various measurement errors in the Homescan data. We organize the discussion around the various dimensions of potential errors we previously discussed: trip information, product (UPC) information, and price/quantity information. We treated the retailer's record as the "truth" and we asked if, or how well, the Homescan record matches it. In that sense, Homescan recording "errors" were defined as records that do not match the retailer's data. Again, to the extent that there are recording errors in the retailer's data, these words should be interpreted accordingly. For example, it could be the case that the retailer's cashier was the one making the error, rather than the Homescan panelist. We think that this latter case is less likely, especially for analysis at the product level and the price and quantity level. At the trip level, when

[7]The discussion assumed that each trip in the Homescan data matched at most one trip in the retailer's data. However, in principle, a trip in the Homescan data might span more than one trip in the retailer's data. This could happen because the consumer remembered an item and went back into the store or because the cashier, for a variety of reasons, closed a transaction in the middle, and had to record a new transaction for a subset of the items purchased. This will most likely show up in our data by having two, or more, trips in the retailer's data that cover a single Homescan record, and would likely lead to an uncertain classification. While there are some examples of such "split trips" in the data, the problem is minor and does not affect the results. Moreover, as long as households always use their loyalty cards, these split trips are not an issue for the second step, where we aggregate all retailer trips to the household-day level. The second step accounts for the majority of the matches.

relying on loyalty card information, it is not clear that the retailer's data were necessarily more accurate. For example, if a household borrows a loyalty card once, then all the shopping trips associated with that card will be linked to the household's record.

Trip Information

There are two types of errors that can be made in recording a trip. First, the household can (correctly) report a trip but misrecord the date or store. This will show up as a Homescan trip that cannot be matched with a trip in the retailer's data. Second, the household can simply not record a trip altogether because the panelist forgot, did not have time, or bought the items and continued elsewhere, so the purchased items never made their way home (where the Homescan scanner resides).

Misrecording

As discussed in the previous section, for each record in the Homescan data we computed two ratios in the data from the first step: r_1 was the fraction of UPCs matched in the trip with the highest UPC overlap, and r_2 was the same ratio for the trip with the second highest UPC overlap. The different panels of figure 2 present the distribution of these two statistics for trips involving different number of distinct UPCs in the Homescan data. In order to display the information, we added a small amount of noise to the data, so that the plotted points can be distinguished from each other. Observations in the lower right corner (high r_1 and low r_2) represent good matches. On the other hand, points in the lower left corner (low r_1, which implies, by construction, low r_2) represent observations that had no match. That is, the Homescan panelist records a trip, but such a trip cannot be found in the store data for that day. Most likely these cases reflect that either the store or date is recorded in error.[8] Observations with intermediate values of r_1 are harder to classify for obvious reasons. Observations in the top right corner (high r_1 and high r_2) also present difficulties: while the high r_1 may suggest a good match, the high value of r_2 suggests that a false positive is also possible.

Overall, there are 2,579 trips that we can potentially match: 579 with 4 or less distinct products (UPCs),[9] 1,191 with more than 4 products but less than 10, and 809 with 10 or more products reported in the Homescan data. Trips with a small number of products, (top left panel, fig. 2) have a large number of cases that are hard to classify. Medium size trips (top right panel) have fewer cases that are uncertain and most of the observations can be mapped into either a reliable match or as unmatchable. For large trips (bottom panel), the separation into reliable matches or unmatchable is clearer.

The left panel of figure 3 displays the (marginal) distribution of r1. The plot makes it clear that the failure in the small trips is not in finding a match, but in finding too many potentially false matches. Almost 80 percent of the small trips have a high r1 compared to roughly 70 percent for medium and large size trips. The problem is that in many of these cases there are other trips in the retailer's data that have a similar number of UPCs matched. These cases have a high probability of producing false matches. This is not surprising. With a small number of products to try to match, it is not likely that we could correctly match a trip. In order to be conservative in our analysis, the

[8]In principle, misrecorded dates could be identified using the data obtained in the second step, which reports all the trips that used the household's loyalty cards. We can then search for a matched trip by the same household without restricting the date to be the same. If the store information is misrecorded, but the retail chain is the same, we can identify such errors in a similar way. We identified in the data such cases (primarily dates that were off by one or two days), but only a relatively small number of them. However, if households who are more likely to misrecord trips are also more likely to misuse their cards, which is consistent with later findings, relying on the second step data to identify misrecorded dates and stores is less useful.

[9]In the data construction process, we restricted Homescan trips to include at least five distinct UPCs. Once we got the data, we tried to match all Homescan trips that could potentially be matched.

small trips are not used. Of course, valid information could be lost. But we preferred to throw away information rather than introduce matching errors.

Looking at figure 2, it seems that for medium and large trips (the top right and bottom panels) there is little information gained by conditioning on r_2 in addition to r_1. This is especially true for large trips where conditional on high levels of r_1 (say, above 0.7), there are almost no observations with r_2 higher than 0.5. This suggests that, unlike the case of small trips, false matches are not a concern. The same is true, but to a lesser degree, with the medium trips.

The distribution presented in figure 3 suggests that since there are few observations for intermediate levels of r_1 there is little to gain by experimenting with different threshold levels of r_1. Therefore, for the analysis that follows below we will look at two sets of trips. The first are large trips with r_1 greater than 0.7. These are the reliable matches. There are 611 such trips. The second set contains medium trips with r_1 greater than 0.7. These are trips that have some chance of being false. We used this set to get an idea of the sensitivity of the findings to matching errors. There are 923 such matches.

The information in figures 2 and 3 can also help address the question of how many of the trips reported in Homescan seem to have misrecorded store and date information. Focusing on large transactions, we find that there are 150 trips with r_1 less than 0.2, 175 with r_1 less than 0.3, and 180 with r_1 less than 0.4 (corresponding to 18.5, 21.6, and 22.4 percent, respectively). For medium trips the corresponding numbers are 113, 155, and 223 (or 9.5, 13.0, and 18.7 percent). Taken together, these numbers suggest that for roughly 20 percent

Figure 2
Match quality in the data from the "first step"

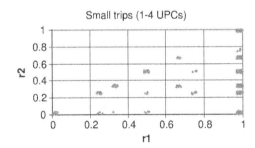

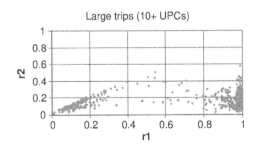

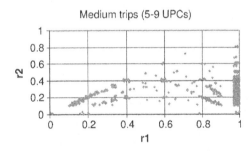

UPCs = universal product codes
r1 and r2 = both ratios of overlapping distinct UPCs in both data sets to the count of distinct UPCs in the Homescan data. r1 is computed for the best match, and r2 is computed for the second best match. Thus, by construction, r2 ≤ r1 ≤ 1.

A good match would have r1 close to 1 and r2 close to 0. When r1 is low, a match is not found. When both r1 and r2 are close to 1, it's hard to classify which of at least two trips (in the retailer's data) is the right match. As the figures show, this last case is never an issue for large trips.

Note:
- UPC counts (used to classify trips as small, medium, or large) are based on the number of distinct UPCs in a trip as reported in the Homescan data.
- Each point in the plot is a potential match: a Homescan trip for which we obtained the entire set of transactions for the same store and day. Some small noise (artificial space) is added to avoid plotting points on top of each other.

Source: Authors' calculations using Homescan and retailer data.

Figure 3
Bimodal distribution of r1

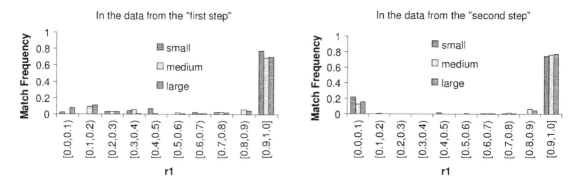

In the data from the "first step"

In the data from the "second step"

r1 and r2 = both ratios of overlapping distinct UPCs in both data sets to the count of distinct UPCs in the Homescan data. r1 is computed for the best match, and r2 is computed for the second best match. Thus, by construction, $r2 \le r1 \le 1$.

Note:
- Universal product code (UPC) counts (which are used to classify trips as small, medium, or large) are based on the number of distinct UPCs in a trip as reported in the Homescan data.
- Each histogram plots the distribution of the r1 statistic. In the "first step," this is the transaction with the highest UPC overlap in the same store and day. In the "second step," this is the specific transaction in the same store and day by the matched household.
- Both histogram show a very clear bimodal pattern, where r1 is either very close to one or very close to zero, and especially so for large trips. This makes it clear why the results remain essentially unchanged when we change the cutoff value of r1 above which we define a match to be successful (throughout the paper we report results that use 0.7 as this cutoff value).

Source: Authors' calculations using Homescan and retailer data.

of the medium and large trips reported in the Homescan data, we can say with a high degree of certainty that they do not match any trip in the retailer's data. Therefore, we concluded that approximately 20 percent of the trips have misrecorded date or store information.[10]

Missed trips

A slightly different way to document errors in recording trip information is to use the retailer's loyalty card information, obtained in the second step, to describe how many trips were not recorded at all by the Homescan households.[11] Recall that the data obtained in the second step include all the trips, according to the retailer, associated with certain households. The data recorded 40,036 trips by the households we asked for during the relevant period. Collapsing these trips by the corresponding Homescan household and the date of the trip, we get 27,746 different trips. Out of these, there were 12,230 trips, roughly 40 percent, that matched a date and store reported in the Homescan data. Out of the 12,230 trips, 5,584 were small, 3,692 were medium, and 2,954 were large, using the definitions in the previous section.

If the way the households are associated with trips was flawless, then the above percentage would give the answer to the question of how many trips were not reported by the Homescan households. However, there are several reasons to believe that the procedure used to get the data generated more trips than the true number of trips by the Homescan households. First, the procedure used to generate the data request for the second step was based on a simple matching algorithm. If this algorithm produces a false match, then we would get several unwanted trips. Second, one could imagine that

[10]Missed or misrecorded trips may bias results of papers that focus, for example, on analyzing store choice (e.g., Katz, 2007).

[11]It is conceivable that these missed trips also represent misrecording of the store information, and would actually show up as a Homescan trip to a different retailer. We tried to look for such trips in the Homescan data with limited success, so are fairly comfortable suggesting that these are likely to be missed, rather than misrecorded, trips.

a household uses a loyalty card that does not belong to them during one of the (correctly) matched trips in the first step. For example, the consumer might borrow a card from a cashier because they did not bring their own. In this case all the trips linked with this card would unjustifiably appear in the second step data. Third, since many households have multiple cards the retailer has a procedure to link all the cards to a household id. This procedure could have generated additional trips that were not made by the Homescan households. Together, these reasons suggest that the above percentage is an overestimate of the number of missed trips.

To improve our estimate of the number of missed trips, we tried to narrow the set of trips by eliminating any trips that potentially suffer from the above mistakes. We did this in several steps. We started by using a similar procedure to that used above, to match the 12,230 trips to trips reported in Homescan. Next, we screened households who generally did not match well with the cards they used. Finally, we re-computed some statistics for the remaining households.

Unlike the data from the first step, the task here is not to find a single trip to match out of many potential trips. Rather, we ask if the trip provided by the retailer for the same household id on the same date seems to be a good match to the corresponding Homescan trip. We only have the data to compute r_1 since in general we have data only for a single trip from the store and date the household claimed to visit. However, the analysis in the previous section suggested that r_1 is sufficient to determine the quality of the match for medium and large trips. We are also less worried about false matches here. In order to generate a false match, two things need to happen. First, at some point the household gets associated with an incorrect card, for any of the reasons mentioned above. Second, the household has to visit the same store on the same day as the true card holder. This coincidence is unlikely.

The right panel of figure 3 displays the distribution of r_1 using the second step data. The distribution is similar to what is shown in the first step data (left panel), but tends to be even more bimodal. Observations either have a very high or very low r_1. As with the first round data, for the analysis that follows below we will look at two sets of trips. The first are reliable matches: large trips with r_1 greater than 0.7. There are 2,537 out of 2,954 (82.5 percent) such trips. The second are matches that have some chance of being false: medium size trips with r_1 greater than 0.7. There are 3,117 out of 3,692 (84.4 percent) such trips. On the other hand, there are roughly 16, 14, and 23 percent of large, medium, and small trips with r_1 less than 0.4.[12] Trips in this category probably have misrecorded store or date, which is quite consistent with the finding in the previous section that approximately 20 percent of the trips have such misrecorded information.

[12]The numbers are essentially the same if we examine cases with r1 less than 0.2.

Having defined matches for the trips, we turn to households. For each of the 291 Homescan households for which we obtained data in the second step, we computed the fraction of their trips that produced a match, where a match is defined as a trip, of any size, with r_1 greater than 0.7. A higher fraction implies that this household made fewer errors in recording the store and date. The distribution of this fraction is displayed in figure 4, for different size trips and overall. We define a poor match as one where the fraction is less than 0.3 (which is between the two modes of the distribution presented in fig. 4).

Figure 4
Distribution of household matches

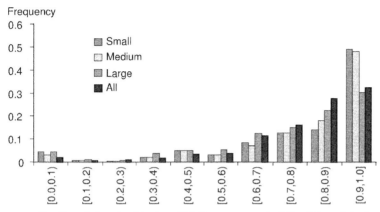

Frequency

Fraction of shopping trips for which Homescan and retailer data matched

Notes:
- A data point in this histogram is a household (based on the Homescan data).
- The histogram plots the fraction of matched trips out of all the trips reported by the household in the Homescan data. It repeats the same exercise for trips of different size (using the Homescan data to define the trip size, as in the earlier figures).
- The figure uses only data from the "second step" (we don't have household identifiers in the retailer data from the "first step"), and shows that for most households we are able to match a fair number of trips. Households with small match rate (less than 0.3) are dropped from most of the analysis in the paper.

Source: Authors' calculations using Homescan and retailer data.

Several of the other households also produce reliable matches a low fraction of the time. However, we want to ignore data from households only if it is fairly certain that these households systematically did not match. This procedure eliminated 18 households and left 273 households.

These 273 households account for 25,732 trips in the retailer's data and 11,478 trips in Homescan. In order to account for the possibility that some households might have occasionally used multiple cards that did not belong to them, we also dropped card numbers that did not have a large fraction of matches (similar to the way we dropped unreliable households.) This left 24,310 transactions in the retailer's data, which yielded 7,321 matches with Homescan trips. On average, across households, this resulted in 53 percent of the trips not being reported in Homescan. There is heterogeneity across households in their accuracy of reporting. In figure 5 we plotted, for these 273 households, the ratio of trips reported in Homescan to the number of trips in the retailer's data (on the horizontal axis) and the fraction of Homescan trips that are matched (on the vertical axis). The plot suggests that there are two types of households. The first group includes those in the upper right corner, who do not miss many trips and also record the trip information fairly accurately. The second group of households is those that either do poorly, or that our matching procedure did not match well. The correlation between the two ratios is 0.47. This suggests that it is more likely that the households, rather than our matching procedure, are those responsible for these poor matches.

Figure 5 is used to classify households as "good" or "bad" depending on how far they are from being perfect matches, which is the point (1,1) in the figure.

Figure 5
Trip statistics

Ratio of matched trips to HS trip count

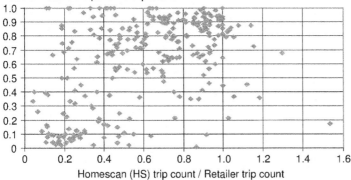

Homescan (HS) trip count / Retailer trip count

Note: - A data point in this histogram is a "good" household as defined in the text. There are 273 such households.
- The horizontal axis reports the ratio between the number of reported Homescan trips and the number of reported retailer trips (based on the retailer's loyalty card use). Ratios below 1 suggest unreported trips (in Homescan). Ratios above 1 suggest trips to the retailer's store without using the loyalty card (or using a card that the retailer did not link to the household).
- The vertical axis reports the fraction of Homescan trip of which we could match a significant number of the universal product codes (UPCs) (at least 0.7).
- A "perfect" household is one for which each of its trips as reported in Homescan is also found in the retailer data, each of its trips as reported by the retailer is found in Homescan, and in all trips a high fraction of UPCs is matched.
- The figure shows a clear distinction between two types of household. Those (the majority of households) which are close to both ratios being 1 report most of their trips, and report the UPCs in each trip relatively well. In contrast, those households that are close to the origin are households that don't report a large fraction of their trips, and don't report (or report incorrectly) many of the UPCs in those trips they do report.
Source: Authors' calculations using Homescan and retailer data.

We then summarize the key characteristics for each group (table 1). One can clearly see that certain demographics are highly correlated with fewer errors. For example, smaller households, and especially households with a single adult seem to be significantly less prone to misrecording trips.

Product Information

We now turn our attention to mistakes in recording items (UPCs) conditional on a trip being matched.[13] Many of these trips did not provide a credible match. In other words, we are unsure that indeed we have the correct trip in the retailer's data. Since we do not want matching errors to affect the findings, the focus was on reliable matches only. We used two different criteria for defining a reliable match. First, we looked at large trips, involving 10 or more products in the Homescan data, with r1 greater than 0.7. There were 2,477 such trips. Second, we examined medium-sized trips, with at least five but no more than nine distinct UPCs in the Homescan data, and with r1 greater than 0.7. There were 3,168 such trips. We did not use the remaining small trips for the rest of the analysis.

Summary statistics for these two groups[14] show that for the typical trip, almost all the products (98 percent in both groups) scanned by the Homescan panelist existed in the retailer's transaction (table 2). Selection into the sample was conditional on this fraction being at least 70 percent (r1>0.7). Nevertheless, we still view this as a remarkably high number. This may not

[13]We have 2,579 matched trips from the first step and 12,230 matched trips from the second step, but there are some trips that appear in the data obtained in both steps, so the total number of matched trips is 13,691.

[14]The classification of a medium trip is based on the (distinct) UPC count at the trip level. The statistics in this table, however, are at the household-date level, which sometimes covers more than a single trip (of a given household in a given day to a given store).

Table 1
Household attributes associated with errors

	"Bad" HH	"Good" HH
HH size	2.50	1.96
HH income	53.82	48.89
No female head of HH	0.05	0.16
Age female	51.63	47.90
No male head of HH	0.21	0.28
Age male	44.90	41.08
Number of children < 18 yrs	0.22	0.13
Number of children < 18 yrs	0.05	0.02
Male employed	0.49	0.47
Male fully employed	0.45	0.42
Female employed	0.50	0.42
Female fully employed	0.38	0.26
Male education	3.30	3.04
Female education	3.92	3.46
Married	0.22	0.42
Non-white	0.13	0.10
"15K" HH	0.08	0.07
Number of observations	129	144

HH = household
"Good" HH is defined as a HH who is - as plotted in Figure 5 - within distance of at most 0.32^0.5 from a "perfect" HH (who is at (1,1)). That is, within a circle that is centered at (1,1) and crosses the point (0.6,0.6) in the figure).

Source: Authors' calculations using Homescan and retailer data.

be surprising, as the products are scanned, so it is, in fact, hard to imagine how misrecording at this level could take place.

On the other hand, there are about 10 percent (14 percent for medium transaction) of the items that show up in the average actual transaction, but are not recorded by the Homescan panelist. Recall that we eliminated from the analysis products with UPCs that only show up in one of the data sets. Thus, these missing items cannot be attributed to categories that the Homescan panelist was not supposed to scan.

We qualitatively tried to analyze which items are more likely to be missing in the Homescan trip, by grouping the missed items into product categories, and investigating whether particular categories stand out. While there were many items that belong to various categories that were occasionally missing, two specific types of items stood out as commonly missing. The first group included consumables: small bottles of drinks, snacks, etc. It seems likely that such items were often consumed on the way home, before the purchase was scanned at home using the Homescan equipment. The second group included items that belong to product categories that include many distinct, yet similar UPCs. Yogurts of different flavors and baby food of different flavors are typical examples. In such cases, it seems likely that individuals simply scanned one of the flavors and entered a large quantity instead of scanning each of the flavors (which would have a distinct UPC) separately. For example, suppose a household buys two yogurts: a strawberry and a vanilla flavor. Each of these has a different UPC, but they have the same price. Instead of scanning each product separately with a quantity of 1, the household might scan one product and enter a quantity of 2. This will appear as a missed product, but in reality might not matter, unless we care about the exact flavor bought. To measure this, we examined the total number of items bought in the trip. In this example, the total quantity would match even if the distinct UPC count did not.[15] This slightly reduces the differences (see table 2), but not by much, implying that misrecorded quantity cannot fully explain the difference in the number of products.

Finally, to get another measure of the importance of the missing items, we compared the total reported expenditure in both the Homescan data and the retailer's data. For large trips, the average Homescan trip reports a higher expenditure despite having a lower number of items. Note, however, that this is driven by some extreme cases since more than half of the matched trips are associated with lower expenditure in Homescan than in the retailer's data (see table 2). In order to check if the mistakes in recording products are systematic, we regressed the missed expenditure on the total trip expenditure and find that a larger fraction of the expenditure was missed on larger trips. This makes sense. On large trips the household is more likely to forget to

[15]These additional results do not account for misrecorded quantities, which is the focus of the next section

Table 2
Summary statistics for matched trips

	Observations	Mean	Standard deviation	5%	25%	50%	75%	95%
			Large trips, r1>=0.7					
Count of distinct UPCs HS	2,477	17.05	7.67	10	11	14	20	33
Count of distinct UPCs R	2,477	19.58	10.81	10	12	16	23	39
UPCs matched / UPCs HS (= "r1")	2,477	0.978	0.069	0.882	1.000	1.000	1.000	1.000
UPCs matched / UPCs R	2,477	0.893	0.160	0.549	0.846	0.941	1.000	1.000
Total number of items HS	2,477	24.75	12.59	12	16	21	30	50
Total number of items R	2,477	26.32	15.77	12	16	22	32	55
Total items HS / total items R	2,477	1.081	0.409	0.783	1.000	1.000	1.067	1.500
Trip expenditure HS (US$)	2,477	53.41	28.79	22.72	33.51	45.18	65.43	111.83
Trip expenditure R (US$)	2,477	53.15	33.03	21.39	31.91	43.51	64.49	114.76
Expenditure HS / expenditure R	2,477	1.024	0.525	0.714	0.857	0.942	1.035	1.474

	Observations	Mean	Standard deviation	5%	25 %	50 %	75%	95%
			Medium trips, r1>=0.7					
Count of distinct UPCs HS[1]	3,168	6.95	2.53	5	5	7	8	9
Count of distinct UPCs R	3,168	9.52	11.36	5	6	7	9	19
UPCs matched / UPCs HS (= "r1")	3,168	0.978	0.082	0.833	1.000	1.000	1.000	1.000
UPCs matched / UPCs R	3,168	0.859	0.214	0.353	0.800	1.000	1.000	1.000
Total number of items HS	3,168	10.54	6.88	5	7	9	12	20
Total number of items R	3,168	13.10	17.85	5	7	10	13	30
Total items HS / total items R	3,168	1.220	0.895	0.800	1.000	1.000	1.111	2.333
Trip expenditure HS (US$)	3,168	22.43	14.01	9.52	14.97	20.10	26.75	41.94
Trip expenditure R (US$)	3,168	26.18	31.46	9.42	14.84	20.02	27.72	59.40
Expenditure HS / expenditure R	3,168	1.120	1.136	0.690	0.866	0.969	1.118	2.357

HS = Homescan data; R = Retailer data
[1]r1 measures the ratio of overlapping distinct UPCs in both data sets to the count of distinct UPCs in the Homescan data for the best match in the data sets. Large and medium trips are defined using the count of distinct UPCs as reported Homescan (medium: 5-9, large: 10+).

Source: Authors' calculations using Homescan and retailer data.

scan, not go through the trouble of doing so, or consume items on the way home.

Price and Quantity Information

We now focus on errors in the price and quantity variables. For this purpose, we looked at the products that appeared in both data sets from the reliably matched trips using the two matching criteria. By presenting the statistics for the two groups separately, we can potentially address the sensitivity of the analysis to matching mistakes. If the statistics are stable across the two groups, it is unlikely that the conclusions we drew were caused by matching mistakes. Indeed, almost all the statistics presented below are similar across the two groups.

For the rest of this section, the first set of matched products, those from trips with more than 10 products and r_1 greater than 0.7, are referred to as "matched large trips," and products matched from medium transactions are referred to as "matched medium trips." For matched large trips, there are 41,158 products purchased, an average of over 17 products per trip. For matched medium trips, there are 21,386 matched items, for an average of almost 7 products per trip (see table 2).

We start by presenting summary statistics for the key variables and then discuss in more detail additional patterns. We calculated the fraction of observations of quantity, expenditure, price, and deal indicator that match between the reports in the Homescan data and in the retailer's data (table 3). For quantity, we find that 94 percent of the time the two data sources reported the same quantity in matched large trips, and 93 percent in matched medium trips.

Next we report the total expenditure on the item, i.e., price multiplied by quantity, and price paid. In the retailer's data two prices are reported: gross and net. The net price is the price paid by the consumer after discounts are applied. We will refer to this as simply the price. This is the price we expect to match the price paid by the Homescan consumer. The gross price is the price pre-discounts. Gross and net expenditure are just these prices multiplied by the retailer reported quantity.[16]

For both groups of trips the frequency that either the expenditure, or price, exactly match is much lower than the matched fraction for the quantity data. The reported expenditure is the same 48 percent of the time, and the price is the same 50 percent of the time. Initially, we believed that expenditure is reported by the households and the price is generated by dividing the expenditure by quantity. If this were the case, then expenditure should be reported more accurately, since price is divided by quantity which introduces an additional error. We were troubled by the finding that prices match slightly better. We currently believe that the price entered in the raw data and the expenditure is then generated, which is consistent with our findings.

The price and expenditure reported in Homescan matches slightly better with the gross price/expenditure, than with the (net, or actual) price/expenditure. Furthermore, the price/expenditure reported in Homescan seems to be between the net and gross reported by the retailer. Originally, we

[16]For about 5 percent of the items, the Homescan data report a positive coupon value. The statistics presented here do not include this value. Adjusting the price paid for the coupon value, or simply focusing on the items that are not associated with a coupon (as reported in Homescan), does not change any of the results.

Table 3
Match statistics for matched trips

	Large trips, r1>=0.7				Medium trips, r1>=0.7			
	Mean	Standard deviation	5%	95%	Mean	Standard deviation	5%	95%
Quantity HS	1.44	1.16	1	3	1.51	1.36	1	4
Quantity R	1.35	0.87	1	3	1.38	0.99	1	3
Same quantity indicator	0.938				0.924			
Expenditure HS	3.14	2.44	0.69	7.38	3.23	2.74	0.69	7.58
Expenditure R	2.76	2.03	0.65	6.00	2.82	2.15	0.66	6.29
Same expenditure indicator	0.479				0.486			
Expenditure R (gross)	3.45	2.48	0.89	7.96	3.56	2.73	0.90	7.98
Same gross exp. indicator	0.619				0.585			
Price HS	2.44	1.63	0.50	4.99	2.44	1.67	0.50	4.99
Price R	2.25	1.53	0.50	4.89	2.27	1.55	0.50	4.99
Same price indicator	0.503				0.512			
Price R (gross)	2.77	1.72	0.67	5.49	2.80	1.79	0.67	5.59
Same gross price indicator	0.651				0.617			
Deal HS	0.520				0.534			
Deal R	0.554				0.549			
Same deal dummy indicator	0.795				0.820			
Observations (UPCs)	41,158				21,386			
Shopping trips	2,477				3,168			
Households	263				318			

HS = Homescan data; R = Retailer data
Large and medium trips are defined using the count of distinct UPCs as reported Homescan (medium: 5-9, large: 10+).
An observations in this table is a distinct item (UPC) in a given trip.

r1 measures the ratio of overlapping distinct UPCs in both data sets to the count of distinct UPCs in the Homescan data for the best match in the data sets. Homescan reports a single price (and a single expenditure). The retailer data reports both net and gross price (and expenditure). We report match statistics by comparing both net and gross variables to the Homescan data.

Source: Authors' calculations using Homescan and retailer data.

were surprised by this finding. However, it is consistent with our current understanding of how the prices are generated. As described earlier, if the consumer purchased the product at a ScanTrack store, i.e., a store for which Nielsen has store-level data, then the Homescan data reports this price, and not the price reported by the consumer. The store-level price is the average transacted price for a given item. If some of the shoppers in that store during that week paid the gross price and some got a discount, then the average would be between the net and the gross, as we found to be true.

Finally, we examine the deal indicator. In the retailer's data, the deal variable equals one if the gross and net price differ. In the Homescan data this is a self reported variable. Even if the price were imputed from the store-level data, the deal indicator is taken from the panelist's report. Overall, the data match in 80 percent of the observations, a worse match than the quantity data, but better than the price data. This is consistent with the price data coming from the aggregate store data, while the deal variable is supposed to match the actual transaction.

On the Accuracy of Nielsen Homescan Data / ERR-69
Economic Research Service/USDA

To better understand the prices and expenditure patterns, we examined the fraction of matches for four different cases, depending on the values of the deal variable in Homescan and the retailer's data (table 4). When both indicators are zero, i.e., both data sets agree that the purchase was not during a sale, (net) price and expenditure match 86 and 83 percent of the time, respectively, in matched large trips, and slightly less in matched medium trips. The match numbers are lower when the retailer indicator is zero while the Homescan

Table 4
Price match statistics, by deal indicator

	Large trips, r1>=0.7					Medium trips, r1>=0.7				
	Observations	Mean	Standard deviations	5%	95%	Obs.	Mean	Standard deviations	5%	95%
Deal: HS=0 and R=0	41,158	0.361				21,386	0.368			
Expenditure HS	14,851	3.01	2.23	0.69	6.78	7,877	2.96	2.28	0.79	6.49
Expenditure R	14,851	3.03	2.10	0.69	6.58	7,877	2.99	2.15	0.79	6.38
Same expenditure indicator	14,851	0.829				7,877	0.816			
Price HS	14,851	2.58	1.63	0.65	4.99	7,877	2.58	1.61	0.65	4.99
Price R	14,851	2.65	1.65	0.69	4.99	7,877	2.66	1.64	0.69	5.39
Same price indicator	14,851	0.856				7,877	0.838			
Deal: HS=1 and R=1	41,158	0.436				21,386	0.453			
Expenditure HS	17,929	3.24	2.58	0.69	7.60	9,681	3.45	3.06	0.69	8.00
Expenditure R	17,929	2.49	1.93	0.50	5.98	9,681	2.62	2.08	0.50	6.00
Same expenditure indicator	17,929	0.252				9,681	0.266			
Expenditure R (gross)	17,929	3.80	2.74	0.99	7.99	9,681	4.04	3.04	0.99	8.99
Same gross expenditure indicator	17,929	0.476				9,681	0.410			
Price HS	17,929	2.36	1.66	0.45	4.99	9,681	2.35	1.73	0.40	4.99
Price R	17,929	1.90	1.35	0.33	3.99	9,681	1.93	1.42	0.40	4.00
Same price indicator	17,929	0.273				9,681	0.294			
Price R (gross)	17,929	2.86	1.80	0.65	5.59	9,681	2.94	1.93	0.67	5.99
Same gross price indicator	17,929	0.510				9,681	0.448			
Deal: HS=1 and R=0	41,158	0.085				21,386	0.082			
Expenditure HS	3,509	2.88	2.41	0.50	6.99	1,758	3.08	2.81	0.50	7.58
Expenditure R	3,509	3.18	2.29	0.79	7.18	1,758	3.41	2.59	0.69	7.70
Same Expenditure Indicator	3,509	0.502				1,758	0.519			
Price HS	3,509	2.19	1.56	0.33	4.75	1,758	2.16	1.47	0.33	4.70
Price R	3,509	2.62	1.68	0.59	5.49	1,758	2.60	1.53	0.50	5.29
Same Price Indicator	3,509	0.548				1,758	0.564			
Deal: HS=0 and R=1	41,158	0.118				21,386	0.097			
Expenditure HS	4,869	3.29	2.53	0.80	7.78	2,070	3.32	2.64	0.79	7.49
Expenditure R	4,869	2.58	1.81	0.60	6.00	2,070	2.61	1.89	0.69	5.49
Same expenditure indicator	4,869	0.228				2,070	0.232			
Expenditure R (gross)	4,869	3.61	2.45	0.99	7.98	2,070	3.62	2.81	0.99	7.98
Same gross expenditure indicator	4,869	0.591				2,070	0.581			
Price HS	4,869	2.53	1.53	0.50	4.99	2,070	2.58	1.69	0.69	4.99
Price R	4,869	2.07	1.31	0.50	4.18	2,070	2.13	1.34	0.50	4.47
Same price indicator	4,869	0.243				2,070	0.247			
Price R (gross)	4,869	2.85	1.61	0.69	5.49	2,070	2.90	1.78	0.79	5.79
Same gross price indicator	4,869	0.623				2,070	0.613			

HS = Homescan data; R = Retailer data
Large and medium trips are defined using the count of distinct UPCs as reported Homescan (medium: 5-9, large: 10+).
An observations in this table is a distinct item (UPC) in a given trip.

r1 measures the ratio of overlapping distinct UPCs in both data sets to the count of distinct UPCs in the Homescan data for the best match in the data sets. Homescan reports a single price (and a single expenditure). The retailer data reports both net and gross price (and expenditure). We report match statistics by comparing both net and gross variables to the Homescan data.

Source: Authors' calculations using Homescan and retailer data.

On the Accuracy of Nielsen Homescan Data / ERR-69
Economic Research Service/USDA

indicator is one. The fraction of matches is significantly lower when we condition on the retailer indicator being equal to one. When the retailer does not have a deal, all the consumers should pay the same price, and therefore the store-level price should equal the price paid by the Homescan consumer. Therefore, it is quite intuitive that prices and expenditures match better (although far from perfect) in this case.

We now explore in more detail the patterns we found for each of the variables. We start with quantity. The overall match rate is reasonable. However, for 73 percent of the Homescan data and 76 percent of the retailer's data (in matched large trips), reported quantities are 1, so a high number of cases where the two quantities are the same might not be surprising. Indeed, conditional on the Homescan data reporting a quantity of 1, the probability of this report matching the retailer's data is 0.99, while conditional of the Homescan data reporting a quantity larger than 1 the probability of a match is only 0.86 (table 5). So a reported quantity of 1 seems to be very reliable, while a quantity greater than 1 might be somewhat more prone to mistakes, but still reasonable. Using the data from the matched large trips, conditional on quantities not matching, 82 percent of the time the quantity reported in Homescan is higher. Recording errors seem to be of various types, including six-packs

Table 5
Quantity matched to quality

q R / q HS	1	2	3	4	5	6	7	8	9	10	12	14	15	16	20	24	30	Total	Same[1]
1	30,014	241	31	20	5	4	0	0	0	0	0	0	0	0	0	0	0	30,315	0.99
2	994	6,792	44	25	5	5	0	1	2	4	2	1	0	0	0	0	0	7,875	0.86
3	171	159	809	19	3	2	1	0	1	0	0	0	0	0	0	0	0	1,165	0.69
4	87	128	37	610	9	4	0	2	0	1	2	0	0	0	0	0	0	880	0.69
5	54	40	14	28	183	9	1	1	0	3	0	0	0	0	0	0	1	334	0.55
6	152	18	15	13	5	127	0	0	0	0	0	0	0	0	0	0	0	330	0.38
7	0	1	1	1	1	1	9	1	0	0	0	0	0	0	0	0	0	15	0.60
8	3	10	1	6	3	1	2	28	0	1	0	0	0	0	0	0	0	55	0.00
9	0	2	0	0	0	0	0	1	2	1	0	0	0	0	0	0	0	6	0.33
10	19	22	10	6	4	2	0	1	1	35	0	0	0	0	0	0	0	100	0.35
11	1	0	0	0	0	0	0	0	0	0	0	0	0	0	0	0	0	1	0.00
12	5	22	1	1	0	0	1	0	0	0	9	0	0	1	0	0	0	40	0.23
13	0	0	0	0	0	0	0	0	0	0	1	0	0	0	0	0	0	1	0.00
15	0	0	1	0	0	0	0	0	0	0	0	0	1	0	0	0	0	2	0.50
16	0	0	0	1	2	0	0	0	0	0	0	0	0	1	0	0	0	4	0.25
17	0	0	0	0	0	0	0	0	0	1	0	0	0	1	0	0	0	2	0.00
18	0	2	1	0	0	0	0	0	0	0	0	0	0	0	0	0	0	3	0.00
20	0	0	0	0	1	0	0	0	0	0	0	0	0	0	1	0	0	2	0.50
24	4	0	0	6	0	0	0	0	0	0	0	0	0	0	0	1	0	11	0.09
25	1	0	0	0	0	0	0	0	0	0	0	0	0	0	0	0	0	1	0.00
30	0	0	0	0	1	0	0	0	0	0	0	0	0	0	0	0	0	1	0.00
48	0	0	0	0	0	0	0	1	0	0	0	0	0	0	0	0	0	1	0.00
Total	31,505	7,437	965	736	222	155	14	36	6	46	14	1	1	3	1	1	1	41,144	
Same[1]	0.95	0.91	0.84	0.83	0.82	0.82	0.64	0.78	0.33	0.76	0.64	0.00	1.00	0.33	1.00	1.00	0.00		0.94

HS = Homescan data; R = Retailer data

An observations in this table is a distinct item (UPC) in a given trip.

[1]"Same" indicates the proportion of cases within the column, row, and overall for which the quantity matches in the two data sets.

Source: Authors' calculations using Homescan and retailer data.

that are recorded as quantities of 6 (the fraction of mistakes for reported quantities of 6, 12, 18 and 24 are 0.60, 0.85, 1.00 and 0.78, respectively), typing errors (the 2 cases of 11 instead of 1), and many others. Some of these mistakes could also be driven by multiple unit packing, and others by similar but not identical items that are counted as the same (as in the yogurt example of the previous section).

We calculated the distribution of the ratio of the log price in the Homescan data to the log of price in the retailer's data (table 6 and figure 6). These statistics confirm what we previously saw. First, the distribution of prices in Homescan is generally between the net and gross prices in the retailer's data. Second, the ratio of prices in the case when both deal indicators are zero is mostly distributed around zero. In other words, even when the price does not match, the differences are small. Third, when the deal indicators are not both zero, the differences can be quite large in the cases where the prices do not match exactly.

In summary, we find that for the matched products, quantity is reported fairly accurately: 94 percent of the quantity information matches in the two data sets, and conditional on a reported quantity of 1 in the Homescan data, this probability went up to 99 percent. Prices and expenditures are reported with less accuracy. In almost half of the cases, the two data sets did not agree. While much of this difference was due to transactions that involved a "deal" in either the Homescan or the retailer's data, even prices that involved no "deal" had recording errors in about 17 percent of the cases. It seems likely that much of the price differences could be attributed to the way Nielsen imputes prices: when available, Nielsen uses store-level prices instead of the actual price paid by the household. Thus, the lower accuracy of the price data may be primarily due to the data construction process. However, this procedure cannot fully explain the difference, as we saw by examining the matching quality when the deal indicators both equal to zero. Finally, the error in the "deal" indicator is smaller than the error in the price. In 80 percent of the cases the "deal" indicator matches the retailer's data.

Table 6
Distribution of log price errors

	Mean	Standard deviation	5%	25%	50%	75%	95%
Overall							
log (price HS / price R)	0.097	0.300	-0.244	0	0	0.223	0.622
log (price HS / price R (gross))	-0.121	0.275	-0.690	-0.118	0	0	0.000
Deal: HS=0 and R=0							
log (price HS / price R)	-0.032	0.152	-0.273	0	0	0	0.000
Deal: HS=1 and R=1							
log (price HS / price R)	0.212	0.343	-0.065	0	0.203	0.402	0.693
log (price HS / price R (gross))	-0.201	0.330	-0.779	-0.336	0	0	0
Deal: HS=1 and R=0							
log (price HS / price R)	-0.075	0.281	-0.691	0	0	0	0.045
Deal: HS=0 and R=1							
log (price HS / price R)	0.202	0.267	-0.004	0	0.179	0.337	0.683
log (price HS / price R (gross))	-0.136	0.251	-0.688	-0.224	0	0	0.000

HS = Homescan data; R = Retailer data
An observation in this table is a distinct item (UPC) in a given trip (number of observations is the same as in table 4).
Homescan reports a single price. The retailer data reports both net and gross price. We report match statistics by comparing both net and gross variables to the Homescan data.

Source: Authors' calculations using Homescan and retailer data.

Figure 6
Kernel densities of log price errors

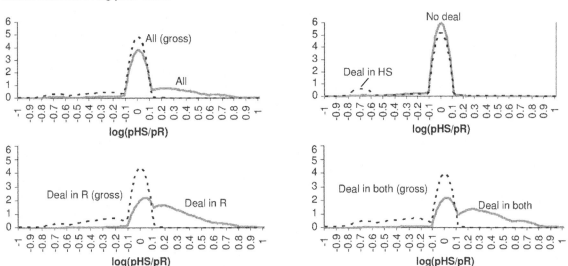

Notes: Each of the plots reports kernel densities of log price differences between the Homescan price (pHS) and the retailer price (pR) for matched items in matched trips.
- The top left panel uses all matches (for net and gross prices as reported by the retailer), the top right panel uses only items for which the retailer had no discounted price (reporting separately cases where Homescan indicates a deal and cases it doesn't), and the bottom panel does it for cases where net and gross prices at the retailer were different (solid lines, which use the net price reported by the retailer, are the more relevant) for cases where Homescan indicates a deal (right) or not (left).
Source: Authors' calculations using Homescan and retailer data.

Do the Differences Matter?

In the previous section, we documented various errors in the Homescan data. The Homescan data are an input into statistical analysis. In principle, even though the data are recorded with error, the analysis could still be mostly unaffected. In this section we ask if the recording errors matter for the conclusions drawn from the analysis. Obviously, the answer depends on the use of the data. We focus on one particular use. Recently, researchers have used Homescan data to study how the prices paid vary with household demographics (e.g., Aguiar and Hurst, 2007). We perform a simple version of such a study in order to evaluate the impact of the errors. Our goal is not to replicate any particular study, but just to investigate whether the errors could have important implications for certain bottom lines.

We present results from a least-squares regression of price paid on household characteristic and UPC fixed effects (table 7). In each set of columns, the first column displays the estimates and the second displays the t-statistics. An observation is a product (UPC) in a matched large trip, i.e., in a large trip with r_l greater than 0.7. The first two columns use as the dependent variable the price, in cents, as recorded in Homescan, and the next two columns use

Table 7

Illustrative analysis of how errors could affect bottom line

Dependent variable	Price (Homescan)		Price (Retailer)		Same sign	Same statistical significance	Coefficient ratio
	Coefficient	t-stat	Coefficient	t-stats			
Constant	286.15	27.39	295.10	9.95			0.97
HH size	-1.32	-2.26	-3.11	0.56	yes	yes	0.42
HH income	0.01	0.86	0.09	0.01	yes	no	0.14
No female head of HH	-41.12	-4.36	-32.85	8.99	yes	yes	1.25
Age female	-1.25	-3.45	-1.71	0.34	yes	yes	0.73
Age female ^ 2	0.01	2.94	0.02	0.00	yes	yes	0.51
No male head of HH	11.51	1.18	-33.06	9.27	no	no	NA
Age male	-0.40	-1.04	-1.34	0.36	yes	no	0.29
Age male ^ 2	0.01	1.37	0.01	0.00	yes	no	0.41
No. of children < 18 yrs	3.42	2.43	1.84	1.34	yes	no	1.87
No. of young children < 6 yrs	-0.81	-0.39	3.61	1.96	no	yes	NA
Male employed	-0.58	-0.27	-11.02	2.08	yes	no	0.05
Male fully employed	5.48	2.64	17.66	1.98	yes	yes	0.31
Female employed	5.26	4.28	1.01	1.17	yes	no	5.18
Female fully employed	-4.08	-3.37	-3.29	1.16	yes	yes	1.24
Male education	1.19	2.69	-1.32	0.42	no	yes	NA
Female education	-1.33	-2.74	1.25	0.46	no	yes	NA
Married	4.79	3.96	1.90	1.15	yes	no	2.52
Non-white	-3.63	-2.35	1.30	1.47	no	no	NA
Hispanic	-3.45	-1.88	-2.99	1.75	yes	yes	1.16
"15K" HH	-1.14	-0.83	-2.47	1.31	yes	yes	0.46
UPC fixed effects	yes		yes				
R^2	0.912		0.910				
Observations	41,158		41,158				

HH = household

An observation in this table is a distinct item (UPC) in a given trip.

The sample used in both regressions is all matched items in the matched large trips.

Regressions include UPC fixed effects, so coefficients indicate the effect of demographics on price paid for an identical item.

Source: Authors' calculations using Homescan and retailer data.

the price in the retailer's data. The last three columns report whether the sign on the coefficients is the same in the two specifications, whether they agree in terms of statistical significance of the coefficient (at a 5-percent confidence level), and the ratio between the coefficient (when the signs agree). Since the regressions include UPC fixed effects, the results tell how the demographics correlate with the price a particular household paid relative to the average (in the sample) price paid for the same item.

The different data give different results. Out of the 20 slope parameters, 5 have different signs, 9 do not agree on their statistical significance, and 13 are statistically different. It is interesting to note that in almost all the cases of statistically significance disagreement, the retailer's data generate significant estimates, while the Homescan data do not. In many cases the difference is also economically meaningful. For example, in the Homescan data the coefficient on race dummy variable is negative and significant, which implies that non-White consumers pay a lower price. On the other hand, in the retailer's data the coefficient is positive but not significant. A researcher using the Homescan data to study discrimination would probably reach different conclusions than one using the retailer's data to study the same question, using the very same set of shopping trips. Another example is in the impact of age on price paid. The Homescan data suggest a flatter impact of age, especially for males, than the retailer's data. Once again researchers using the data to study life cycle consumption might reach wrong conclusion using the Homescan data.

There are two factors that cause the difference in the results. First, Nielsen imputes store level prices for many of the observations. Suppose that all the price information in the Homescan data were imputed and consider, for example, the race dummy variable. In this case, the regression using the Homescan data shows that non-White households tend to buy at cheaper stores, i.e., stores where the average consumer in the store pays less for the same item. The regression using the retailer's data tells us that despite going to cheaper stores non-White panelists do not pay less on average.

A second reason for the difference in the results is due to recording errors. Suppose that none of the prices are imputed and the only difference is due to recording mistakes made by the panelist. Once again, we use the race dummy variables as an example. The regression using the Homescan data tells us that nonwhite consumers report a lower price. On the other hand, the regression using the retailer's data suggests that those consumers do not actually pay less, maybe even slightly more. Together these suggest that White consumers tend to over-report prices relative to non-White consumers, not that the White consumers are likely to pay more.

Conclusions

This analysis suggests that the Homescan data contain recording errors in several dimensions, but that the overall accuracy of self-reported data by Homescan panelists seems to be in line with many other surveys of this type. Our research fits into a broader literature of validation studies that have been conducted in the economics literature since responses to surveys and self-reported data are the foundation of many data sets used by economic researchers and policymakers. For example, the Panel Study of Income Dynamics (PSID), the Current Population Survey (CPS), and the Consumer Expenditure Survey (CEX) all include self-reported data and are used heavily by economists. One concern in using self-reported data is that information is recorded with error, and that the error is systematically related to the characteristics of the respondents or to the variables being recorded. To study the magnitude of measurement error and to document the distribution of the error, an empirical literature has emerged that compares the self-reported sample to a validation study.[17] While most of the literature has focused on data sets that record labor market decisions and outcomes, the Homescan data focuses on food purchase decisions. We compared the recording errors we find here to errors in these commonly used economic data sets and find that errors in Homescan are of the same order of magnitude as errors in earnings and employment-status data.

[17]Bound at el. (2001) provide a detailed review of this literature.

Having the unique opportunity to cross-validate a sub-sample of the Homescan data with retailer data allowed us to identify data misrecordings that would usually go undetected in most data sets and surveys. The most concerning issue we find relates to the way that prices are recorded by Nielsen for stores from which Nielsen uses its store-level data as an estimate of what households actually paid. This poses additional challenges when those stores have multiple possible prices in a given time period due to loyalty card or other shopper-specific price promotions.

We now offer some thoughts on what could be done to improve the data. Since prices are the variable most poorly recorded due, at least in part, to the way Nielsen imputes store-level prices, it seems that, at the very least, the data should include an indicator that an imputed price is used for a given shopping trip. Ideally, it would be best to know both the imputed store-level price and the price reported by the household. This information is not currently collected by Nielsen, but collecting this information, at least on an experimental basis, would allow for additional analysis of the magnitude of this discrepancy. There is still good reason to use store-level prices, when available as that additional information can be used, for example, to better identify purchases on deal. A deal can then be defined as any situation in which the price reported by the consumer is less than the store non-deal price reported by the store.

Nielsen could also probably improve the quality of the data by requiring the panelists to send in their receipts. The reported data could then be compared to those receipts (at least one other consumer panel-level data that uses this procedure). Random sampling of the receipts will both make the panelists more careful, and would also allow for quality control. As we find that certain households are more prone to mistakes along all the dimensions we analyzed, such random sampling may be used to design better sampling weights, or even to drop out of the sample "negligent" panelists. The final analysis of the data can be improved, and bias potentially removed, by constructing a reliability index for the observations and weighting them accordingly. Given the current data available in Homescan, such an index might be hard to construct. But future data collection can be done with this goal in mind.

References

Aguiar, Mark, and Erik Hurst. 2007. "Life-Cycle Prices and Production," *American Economic Review* 97(5), pp. 1533-1559.

Bound, John, Charles C. Brown, and Nancy Mathiowetz. 2001. "Measurement Error in Survey Data," *Handbook of Econometrics*, edited by E.E. Learner and J.J. Heckman, pp. 3705-3843. New York: North Holland Publishing.

Broda, Christian, and David E. Weinstein. 2007. "Understanding International Price Differences Using Barcode Data." Working paper. University of Chicago, Graduate School of Business.

Hausman, J., and E. Leibtag. 2007. "Consumer Benefits from Increased Competition in Shopping Outlets: Measuring the Effect of Wal-Mart," *Journal of Applied Econometrics*. Vol. 22, No. 7: 1157-77.

Katz, Michael. 2007. "Estimating Supermarket Choice using Moment Inequalities." Mimeo. Harvard University, Cambridge, MA.

Nielsen Homescan Data, ERS-USDA version, 2004. Additional information on this data can be found at http://www.nielsen.com/clients/index.html.

Retail Scan Data, private data accessed through a data-sharing agreement with Stanford University, 2004.

CPSIA information can be obtained at www.ICGtesting.com
Printed in the USA
BVOW08s1118031014

369390BV00013B/222/P